50 Smoothies for Every Season
Recipes for Summer

By: Kelly Johnson

Table of Contents

Spring Smoothies

1. Strawberry Banana Smoothie
2. Peach and Spinach Smoothie
3. Pineapple Coconut Smoothie
4. Mango Mint Smoothie
5. Avocado Citrus Smoothie
6. Kiwi and Spinach Smoothie
7. Cucumber Melon Smoothie
8. Berry Basil Smoothie
9. Green Apple Kale Smoothie
10. Carrot Ginger Smoothie

Summer Smoothies

11. Watermelon Berry Smoothie
12. Tropical Paradise Smoothie (Mango, Pineapple, Coconut)
13. Blueberry Lemonade Smoothie
14. Peach and Raspberry Smoothie
15. Chocolate Banana Nut Smoothie
16. Pineapple Orange Smoothie
17. Strawberry Mango Smoothie
18. Coconut Lime Smoothie
19. Cherry Limeade Smoothie
20. Dragon Fruit Smoothie

Autumn Smoothies

21. Pumpkin Spice Smoothie
22. Apple Cinnamon Smoothie
23. Maple Pecan Smoothie

24. Caramel Apple Smoothie
25. Sweet Potato and Banana Smoothie
26. Cranberry Orange Smoothie
27. Pecan Pie Smoothie
28. Fall Harvest Smoothie (Squash, Apple, and Cinnamon)
29. Chai Spice Smoothie
30. Spiced Pear Smoothie

Winter Smoothies

31. Chocolate Peppermint Smoothie
32. Orange Creamsicle Smoothie
33. Cinnamon Roll Smoothie
34. Warm Gingerbread Smoothie
35. Cocoa Almond Smoothie
36. Banana Nutmeg Smoothie
37. Hot Chocolate Smoothie
38. Berry Chai Smoothie
39. Cranberry Almond Smoothie
40. Spiced Pumpkin Smoothie

Year-Round Favorites

41. Green Protein Smoothie (Spinach, Protein Powder, Banana)
42. Peanut Butter Banana Smoothie
43. Mango Green Smoothie
44. Chocolate Avocado Smoothie
45. Berry Protein Smoothie
46. Superfood Smoothie (with Chia Seeds and Spinach)
47. Tropical Green Smoothie (with Kale and Pineapple)
48. Honeydew Mint Smoothie
49. Nutty Banana Oatmeal Smoothie
50. Matcha Berry Smoothie

Spring Smoothies

Strawberry Banana Smoothie

Ingredients:

- 1 cup fresh or frozen strawberries
- 1 ripe banana
- 1 cup yogurt (plain or flavored)
- 1/2 cup milk (dairy or non-dairy)
- 1 tablespoon honey or maple syrup (optional)
- Ice cubes (optional)

Instructions:

1. In a blender, combine strawberries, banana, yogurt, milk, and honey or maple syrup if using.
2. Blend until smooth. If you prefer a thicker smoothie, add ice cubes and blend again.
3. Pour into glasses and enjoy immediately.

Peach and Spinach Smoothie

Ingredients:

- 1 cup fresh or frozen peaches
- 1 cup fresh spinach leaves
- 1/2 banana (optional)
- 1 cup almond milk (or your choice of milk)
- 1 tablespoon chia seeds (optional)
- Ice cubes (optional)

Instructions:

1. Place peaches, spinach, banana (if using), almond milk, and chia seeds in a blender.
2. Blend until smooth, adding ice cubes for a colder, thicker texture if desired.
3. Pour into a glass and enjoy.

Pineapple Coconut Smoothie

Ingredients:

- 1 cup fresh or frozen pineapple chunks
- 1/2 cup coconut milk (canned or carton)
- 1/2 cup yogurt (coconut or regular)
- 1 tablespoon shredded coconut (optional)
- Ice cubes (optional)

Instructions:

1. In a blender, combine pineapple, coconut milk, yogurt, and shredded coconut if using.
2. Blend until creamy and smooth. Add ice cubes if you want a colder smoothie.
3. Serve immediately, garnished with additional shredded coconut if desired.

Mango Mint Smoothie

Ingredients:

- 1 ripe mango, peeled and chopped
- 1/2 cup fresh mint leaves
- 1 cup yogurt (plain or flavored)
- 1 cup coconut water or regular water
- 1 tablespoon honey or agave syrup (optional)

Instructions:

1. Add mango, mint leaves, yogurt, coconut water, and honey or agave syrup to a blender.
2. Blend until smooth. Adjust consistency with more water if needed.
3. Pour into a glass and enjoy fresh and refreshing.

Avocado Citrus Smoothie

Ingredients:

- 1 ripe avocado, peeled and pitted
- 1 orange, peeled and segmented
- 1/2 lemon or lime, juiced
- 1 cup spinach or kale (optional)
- 1 cup almond milk (or your choice of milk)
- Honey or maple syrup to taste (optional)

Instructions:

1. In a blender, combine avocado, orange, lemon or lime juice, spinach or kale (if using), and almond milk.
2. Blend until smooth. Taste and add honey or maple syrup if desired for sweetness.
3. Serve immediately, garnished with a slice of citrus if desired.

Enjoy these delicious and healthy smoothies!

Kiwi and Spinach Smoothie

Ingredients:

- 2 ripe kiwis, peeled and chopped
- 1 cup fresh spinach leaves
- 1 banana
- 1/2 cup yogurt (plain or flavored)
- 1 cup coconut water or water
- Ice cubes (optional)

Instructions:

1. In a blender, combine kiwis, spinach, banana, yogurt, and coconut water.
2. Blend until smooth. Add ice cubes for a thicker texture if desired.
3. Pour into a glass and enjoy immediately.

Cucumber Melon Smoothie

Ingredients:

- 1 cup cucumber, peeled and chopped
- 1 cup cantaloupe or honeydew melon, chopped
- 1/2 lime, juiced
- 1 cup coconut water or regular water
- Fresh mint leaves (optional)

Instructions:

1. Place cucumber, melon, lime juice, and coconut water in a blender.
2. Blend until smooth. Add mint leaves for extra flavor if desired.
3. Serve chilled, garnished with additional cucumber or melon slices.

Berry Basil Smoothie

Ingredients:

- 1 cup mixed berries (strawberries, blueberries, raspberries)
- 1/4 cup fresh basil leaves
- 1 banana
- 1 cup yogurt (plain or flavored)
- 1/2 cup almond milk (or your choice of milk)

Instructions:

1. In a blender, combine berries, basil, banana, yogurt, and almond milk.
2. Blend until smooth. Adjust consistency by adding more almond milk if needed.
3. Serve immediately, garnished with a few whole berries and basil leaves.

Green Apple Kale Smoothie

Ingredients:

- 1 green apple, cored and chopped
- 1 cup kale leaves, stems removed
- 1/2 banana
- 1 cup almond milk (or your choice of milk)
- 1 tablespoon honey or agave syrup (optional)

Instructions:

1. Combine apple, kale, banana, almond milk, and honey in a blender.
2. Blend until smooth. Adjust sweetness if desired by adding more honey or agave syrup.
3. Pour into a glass and enjoy the refreshing taste.

Carrot Ginger Smoothie

Ingredients:

- 1 cup carrots, peeled and chopped
- 1/2 inch fresh ginger, peeled and grated
- 1 banana
- 1 cup orange juice
- 1/2 cup yogurt (plain or flavored)

Instructions:

1. In a blender, combine carrots, ginger, banana, orange juice, and yogurt.
2. Blend until smooth and creamy. Adjust consistency with more orange juice if needed.
3. Serve chilled, garnished with a carrot stick or a sprinkle of ginger.

Summer Smoothies

Watermelon Berry Smoothie

Ingredients:

- 2 cups watermelon, cubed and seeds removed
- 1 cup mixed berries (strawberries, blueberries, raspberries)
- 1/2 cup yogurt (plain or flavored)
- 1 tablespoon honey or maple syrup (optional)
- Ice cubes (optional)

Instructions:

1. In a blender, combine watermelon, mixed berries, yogurt, and honey or maple syrup if using.
2. Blend until smooth. Add ice cubes for a colder, thicker texture if desired.
3. Pour into glasses and enjoy immediately.

Tropical Paradise Smoothie (Mango, Pineapple, Coconut)

Ingredients:

- 1 cup mango chunks (fresh or frozen)
- 1 cup pineapple chunks (fresh or frozen)
- 1/2 cup coconut milk (canned or carton)
- 1/2 cup yogurt (coconut or regular)
- 1 tablespoon shredded coconut (optional)

Instructions:

1. In a blender, combine mango, pineapple, coconut milk, yogurt, and shredded coconut if using.
2. Blend until smooth and creamy. Adjust consistency with more coconut milk if needed.
3. Serve immediately, garnished with additional shredded coconut if desired.

Blueberry Lemonade Smoothie

Ingredients:

- 1 cup fresh or frozen blueberries
- 1/2 cup lemonade (store-bought or homemade)
- 1/2 banana (optional)
- 1/2 cup yogurt (plain or flavored)
- Ice cubes (optional)

Instructions:

1. In a blender, combine blueberries, lemonade, banana (if using), and yogurt.
2. Blend until smooth. Add ice cubes for a chilled smoothie if desired.
3. Pour into glasses and enjoy the refreshing flavor.

Peach and Raspberry Smoothie

Ingredients:

- 1 cup fresh or frozen peaches, chopped
- 1 cup fresh or frozen raspberries
- 1 cup almond milk (or your choice of milk)
- 1/2 cup yogurt (plain or flavored)
- Honey or agave syrup to taste (optional)

Instructions:

1. In a blender, combine peaches, raspberries, almond milk, and yogurt.
2. Blend until smooth. Taste and add honey or agave syrup for sweetness if desired.
3. Serve immediately, garnished with fresh raspberries or peach slices.

Chocolate Banana Nut Smoothie

Ingredients:

- 1 ripe banana
- 1 tablespoon cocoa powder
- 1 tablespoon peanut butter or almond butter
- 1 cup almond milk (or your choice of milk)
- 1 tablespoon honey or maple syrup (optional)
- Ice cubes (optional)

Instructions:

1. In a blender, combine banana, cocoa powder, nut butter, almond milk, and honey or maple syrup if using.
2. Blend until smooth and creamy. Add ice cubes for a colder smoothie if desired.
3. Pour into a glass and enjoy the rich chocolate flavor.

Enjoy these delicious and refreshing smoothies!

Pineapple Orange Smoothie

Ingredients:

- 1 cup fresh or frozen pineapple chunks
- 1 orange, peeled and segmented
- 1/2 banana (optional)
- 1 cup coconut water or almond milk
- Ice cubes (optional)

Instructions:

1. In a blender, combine pineapple, orange, banana (if using), and coconut water or almond milk.
2. Blend until smooth. Add ice cubes for a colder, thicker texture if desired.
3. Pour into glasses and enjoy immediately.

Strawberry Mango Smoothie

Ingredients:

- 1 cup fresh or frozen strawberries
- 1 cup fresh or frozen mango chunks
- 1 cup yogurt (plain or flavored)
- 1/2 cup orange juice
- Ice cubes (optional)

Instructions:

1. In a blender, combine strawberries, mango, yogurt, and orange juice.
2. Blend until smooth. Add ice cubes for a chilled smoothie if desired.
3. Serve immediately, garnished with fresh strawberries or mango slices.

Coconut Lime Smoothie

Ingredients:

- 1 cup coconut milk (canned or carton)
- 1/2 cup yogurt (coconut or regular)
- Zest and juice of 1 lime
- 1 tablespoon honey or agave syrup (optional)
- Ice cubes (optional)

Instructions:

1. In a blender, combine coconut milk, yogurt, lime zest, lime juice, and honey or agave syrup if using.
2. Blend until smooth. Add ice cubes for a colder smoothie if desired.
3. Pour into glasses and enjoy the tropical flavor.

Cherry Limeade Smoothie

Ingredients:

- 1 cup fresh or frozen cherries, pitted
- Juice of 1 lime
- 1/2 cup lemonade (store-bought or homemade)
- 1 cup almond milk (or your choice of milk)
- Ice cubes (optional)

Instructions:

1. In a blender, combine cherries, lime juice, lemonade, and almond milk.
2. Blend until smooth. Add ice cubes for a chilled smoothie if desired.
3. Serve immediately, garnished with a cherry or lime wedge.

Dragon Fruit Smoothie

Ingredients:

- 1 cup dragon fruit (fresh or frozen), peeled and chopped
- 1 banana
- 1/2 cup coconut milk or yogurt
- 1 tablespoon honey or agave syrup (optional)
- Ice cubes (optional)

Instructions:

1. In a blender, combine dragon fruit, banana, coconut milk or yogurt, and honey or agave syrup if using.
2. Blend until smooth. Add ice cubes for a colder, thicker texture if desired.
3. Pour into glasses and enjoy the vibrant color and taste.

Enjoy these refreshing and delicious smoothies!

Autumn Smoothies

Pumpkin Spice Smoothie

Ingredients:

- 1 cup canned pumpkin puree
- 1 banana
- 1 cup almond milk (or your choice of milk)
- 1/2 teaspoon pumpkin pie spice
- 1 tablespoon maple syrup (or honey)
- Ice cubes (optional)

Instructions:

1. In a blender, combine pumpkin puree, banana, almond milk, pumpkin pie spice, and maple syrup.
2. Blend until smooth. Add ice cubes for a colder smoothie if desired.
3. Serve immediately, garnished with a sprinkle of pumpkin pie spice on top.

Apple Cinnamon Smoothie

Ingredients:

- 1 apple, cored and chopped (skin on)
- 1/2 banana
- 1 cup almond milk (or your choice of milk)
- 1/2 teaspoon cinnamon
- 1 tablespoon honey or maple syrup (optional)
- Ice cubes (optional)

Instructions:

1. In a blender, combine apple, banana, almond milk, cinnamon, and honey or maple syrup if using.
2. Blend until smooth. Add ice cubes for a chilled smoothie if desired.
3. Pour into glasses and enjoy immediately.

Maple Pecan Smoothie

Ingredients:

- 1/4 cup pecans (toasted if desired)
- 1 banana
- 1 cup almond milk (or your choice of milk)
- 1 tablespoon maple syrup
- 1/2 teaspoon vanilla extract
- Ice cubes (optional)

Instructions:

1. In a blender, combine pecans, banana, almond milk, maple syrup, and vanilla extract.
2. Blend until smooth. Add ice cubes for a colder smoothie if desired.
3. Serve immediately, garnished with chopped pecans.

Caramel Apple Smoothie

Ingredients:

- 1 apple, cored and chopped (skin on)
- 1 banana
- 1 cup almond milk (or your choice of milk)
- 2 tablespoons caramel sauce (plus extra for drizzling)
- 1/2 teaspoon cinnamon
- Ice cubes (optional)

Instructions:

1. In a blender, combine apple, banana, almond milk, caramel sauce, and cinnamon.
2. Blend until smooth. Add ice cubes for a chilled smoothie if desired.
3. Serve in a glass drizzled with additional caramel sauce.

Sweet Potato and Banana Smoothie

Ingredients:

- 1/2 cup cooked sweet potato (cooled)
- 1 banana
- 1 cup almond milk (or your choice of milk)
- 1/2 teaspoon cinnamon
- 1 tablespoon maple syrup (or honey)
- Ice cubes (optional)

Instructions:

1. In a blender, combine sweet potato, banana, almond milk, cinnamon, and maple syrup.
2. Blend until smooth. Add ice cubes for a colder smoothie if desired.
3. Pour into glasses and enjoy immediately.

Cranberry Orange Smoothie

Ingredients:

- 1 cup fresh or frozen cranberries
- 1 orange, peeled and segmented
- 1/2 banana
- 1 cup almond milk (or your choice of milk)
- 1 tablespoon honey or maple syrup (optional)

Instructions:

1. In a blender, combine cranberries, orange, banana, almond milk, and honey or maple syrup if using.
2. Blend until smooth. Adjust sweetness if desired.
3. Serve immediately, garnished with a few whole cranberries or an orange slice.

Enjoy these seasonal and flavorful smoothies!

Pecan Pie Smoothie

Ingredients:

- 1/4 cup pecans (toasted if desired)
- 1 banana
- 1 cup almond milk (or your choice of milk)
- 1 tablespoon maple syrup
- 1/2 teaspoon vanilla extract
- 1/2 teaspoon cinnamon
- Ice cubes (optional)

Instructions:

1. In a blender, combine pecans, banana, almond milk, maple syrup, vanilla extract, and cinnamon.
2. Blend until smooth. Add ice cubes for a chilled smoothie if desired.
3. Serve immediately, garnished with chopped pecans and a sprinkle of cinnamon.

Fall Harvest Smoothie (Squash, Apple, and Cinnamon)

Ingredients:

- 1/2 cup cooked and cooled butternut squash (or pumpkin)
- 1 apple, cored and chopped
- 1 cup almond milk (or your choice of milk)
- 1/2 teaspoon cinnamon
- 1 tablespoon maple syrup (or honey)
- Ice cubes (optional)

Instructions:

1. In a blender, combine butternut squash, apple, almond milk, cinnamon, and maple syrup.
2. Blend until smooth. Add ice cubes for a colder smoothie if desired.
3. Pour into glasses and enjoy immediately.

Chai Spice Smoothie

Ingredients:

- 1 banana
- 1 cup almond milk (or your choice of milk)
- 1/2 teaspoon chai spice blend (or a mix of cinnamon, ginger, and cardamom)
- 1 tablespoon maple syrup (or honey)
- 1 tablespoon chia seeds (optional)
- Ice cubes (optional)

Instructions:

1. In a blender, combine banana, almond milk, chai spice blend, maple syrup, and chia seeds if using.
2. Blend until smooth. Add ice cubes for a chilled smoothie if desired.
3. Serve immediately, garnished with a sprinkle of cinnamon or extra chai spice.

Spiced Pear Smoothie

Ingredients:

- 1 ripe pear, cored and chopped
- 1/2 banana
- 1 cup almond milk (or your choice of milk)
- 1/2 teaspoon cinnamon
- 1 tablespoon honey or maple syrup (optional)
- Ice cubes (optional)

Instructions:

1. In a blender, combine pear, banana, almond milk, cinnamon, and honey or maple syrup if using.
2. Blend until smooth. Add ice cubes for a colder smoothie if desired.
3. Pour into glasses and enjoy immediately.

Enjoy these delicious and cozy smoothies perfect for fall!

Winter Smoothies

Chocolate Peppermint Smoothie

Ingredients:

- 1 banana
- 1 cup almond milk (or your choice of milk)
- 2 tablespoons cocoa powder
- 1/2 teaspoon peppermint extract
- 1 tablespoon maple syrup (or honey)
- Ice cubes (optional)

Instructions:

1. In a blender, combine banana, almond milk, cocoa powder, peppermint extract, and maple syrup.
2. Blend until smooth. Add ice cubes for a chilled smoothie if desired.
3. Serve immediately, garnished with crushed peppermint candy if desired.

Orange Creamsicle Smoothie

Ingredients:

- 1 orange, peeled and segmented
- 1/2 banana
- 1 cup yogurt (vanilla or plain)
- 1/2 cup almond milk (or your choice of milk)
- 1 tablespoon honey or maple syrup (optional)

Instructions:

1. In a blender, combine orange, banana, yogurt, almond milk, and honey or maple syrup if using.
2. Blend until smooth. Adjust sweetness if desired.
3. Pour into glasses and enjoy immediately.

Cinnamon Roll Smoothie

Ingredients:

- 1 banana
- 1 cup almond milk (or your choice of milk)
- 1/2 teaspoon cinnamon
- 1 tablespoon maple syrup (or honey)
- 1 tablespoon rolled oats
- Ice cubes (optional)

Instructions:

1. In a blender, combine banana, almond milk, cinnamon, maple syrup, and rolled oats.
2. Blend until smooth. Add ice cubes for a colder smoothie if desired.
3. Serve immediately, garnished with a sprinkle of cinnamon.

Warm Gingerbread Smoothie

Ingredients:

- 1 banana
- 1 cup almond milk (or your choice of milk)
- 1/2 teaspoon gingerbread spice blend (or a mix of ginger, cinnamon, and nutmeg)
- 1 tablespoon molasses
- 1 tablespoon maple syrup (or honey)

Instructions:

1. In a blender, combine banana, almond milk, gingerbread spice blend, molasses, and maple syrup.
2. Blend until smooth. For a warm smoothie, heat the mixture in a saucepan until warm, then pour into glasses.
3. Serve immediately.

Cocoa Almond Smoothie

Ingredients:

- 1 banana
- 1 cup almond milk (or your choice of milk)
- 2 tablespoons cocoa powder
- 1 tablespoon almond butter
- 1 tablespoon maple syrup (or honey)
- Ice cubes (optional)

Instructions:

1. In a blender, combine banana, almond milk, cocoa powder, almond butter, and maple syrup.
2. Blend until smooth. Add ice cubes for a chilled smoothie if desired.
3. Serve immediately, garnished with sliced almonds.

Banana Nutmeg Smoothie

Ingredients:

- 1 banana
- 1 cup almond milk (or your choice of milk)
- 1/2 teaspoon nutmeg
- 1 tablespoon maple syrup (or honey)
- Ice cubes (optional)

Instructions:

1. In a blender, combine banana, almond milk, nutmeg, and maple syrup.
2. Blend until smooth. Add ice cubes for a colder smoothie if desired.
3. Serve immediately, garnished with a sprinkle of nutmeg.

Hot Chocolate Smoothie

Ingredients:

- 1 banana
- 1 cup almond milk (or your choice of milk)
- 2 tablespoons cocoa powder
- 1 tablespoon maple syrup (or honey)
- 1/2 teaspoon vanilla extract
- Ice cubes (optional)

Instructions:

1. In a blender, combine banana, almond milk, cocoa powder, maple syrup, and vanilla extract.
2. Blend until smooth. For a hot smoothie, heat the mixture in a saucepan until warm, then pour into glasses.
3. Serve immediately, topped with whipped cream if desired.

Enjoy these indulgent and flavorful smoothies!

Berry Chai Smoothie

Ingredients:

- 1 cup mixed berries (fresh or frozen)
- 1 banana
- 1 cup almond milk (or your choice of milk)
- 1/2 teaspoon chai spice blend (or a mix of cinnamon, ginger, and cardamom)
- 1 tablespoon honey or maple syrup (optional)
- Ice cubes (optional)

Instructions:

1. In a blender, combine mixed berries, banana, almond milk, chai spice blend, and honey or maple syrup if using.
2. Blend until smooth. Add ice cubes for a colder smoothie if desired.
3. Serve immediately, garnished with a few whole berries.

Cranberry Almond Smoothie

Ingredients:

- 1 cup fresh or frozen cranberries
- 1 banana
- 1 cup almond milk (or your choice of milk)
- 2 tablespoons almond butter
- 1 tablespoon honey or maple syrup (optional)

Instructions:

1. In a blender, combine cranberries, banana, almond milk, almond butter, and honey or maple syrup if using.
2. Blend until smooth. Adjust sweetness if desired.
3. Serve immediately, garnished with sliced almonds or whole cranberries.

Spiced Pumpkin Smoothie

Ingredients:

- 1/2 cup canned pumpkin puree
- 1 banana
- 1 cup almond milk (or your choice of milk)
- 1/2 teaspoon pumpkin pie spice
- 1 tablespoon maple syrup (or honey)
- Ice cubes (optional)

Instructions:

1. In a blender, combine pumpkin puree, banana, almond milk, pumpkin pie spice, and maple syrup.
2. Blend until smooth. Add ice cubes for a chilled smoothie if desired.
3. Serve immediately, garnished with a sprinkle of pumpkin pie spice.

Enjoy these delicious and festive smoothies!

Year-Round Favorites

Green Protein Smoothie

Ingredients:

- 1 cup fresh spinach
- 1 banana
- 1 scoop protein powder (vanilla or unflavored)
- 1 cup almond milk (or your choice of milk)
- Ice cubes (optional)

Instructions:

1. In a blender, combine spinach, banana, protein powder, and almond milk.
2. Blend until smooth. Add ice cubes for a colder smoothie if desired.
3. Serve immediately, garnished with a few spinach leaves or a sprinkle of protein powder.

Peanut Butter Banana Smoothie

Ingredients:

- 1 banana
- 1 cup almond milk (or your choice of milk)
- 2 tablespoons peanut butter
- 1 tablespoon honey or maple syrup (optional)
- Ice cubes (optional)

Instructions:

1. In a blender, combine banana, almond milk, peanut butter, and honey or maple syrup if using.
2. Blend until smooth. Add ice cubes for a chilled smoothie if desired.
3. Serve immediately, garnished with banana slices or a drizzle of peanut butter.

Mango Green Smoothie

Ingredients:

- 1 cup fresh spinach
- 1 cup mango chunks (fresh or frozen)
- 1 banana
- 1 cup coconut water (or your choice of liquid)
- Ice cubes (optional)

Instructions:

1. In a blender, combine spinach, mango chunks, banana, and coconut water.
2. Blend until smooth. Add ice cubes for a colder smoothie if desired.
3. Serve immediately, garnished with a few mango pieces or spinach leaves.

Chocolate Avocado Smoothie

Ingredients:

- 1 ripe avocado
- 1 banana
- 1 cup almond milk (or your choice of milk)
- 2 tablespoons cocoa powder
- 1 tablespoon honey or maple syrup (optional)
- Ice cubes (optional)

Instructions:

1. In a blender, combine avocado, banana, almond milk, cocoa powder, and honey or maple syrup if using.
2. Blend until smooth. Add ice cubes for a chilled smoothie if desired.
3. Serve immediately, garnished with cocoa powder or chocolate shavings.

Berry Protein Smoothie

Ingredients:

- 1 cup mixed berries (fresh or frozen)
- 1 banana
- 1 scoop protein powder (vanilla or berry-flavored)
- 1 cup almond milk (or your choice of milk)
- Ice cubes (optional)

Instructions:

1. In a blender, combine mixed berries, banana, protein powder, and almond milk.
2. Blend until smooth. Add ice cubes for a colder smoothie if desired.
3. Serve immediately, garnished with a few whole berries or a sprinkle of protein powder.

Superfood Smoothie (with Chia Seeds and Spinach)

Ingredients:

- 1 cup fresh spinach
- 1 banana
- 1 tablespoon chia seeds
- 1 cup almond milk (or your choice of milk)
- 1 tablespoon honey or maple syrup (optional)
- Ice cubes (optional)

Instructions:

1. In a blender, combine spinach, banana, chia seeds, almond milk, and honey or maple syrup if using.
2. Blend until smooth. Add ice cubes for a chilled smoothie if desired.
3. Serve immediately, garnished with a sprinkle of chia seeds or spinach leaves.

Enjoy these nutritious and delicious smoothies!

Tropical Green Smoothie (with Kale and Pineapple)

Ingredients:

- 1 cup fresh kale, stems removed
- 1 cup pineapple chunks (fresh or frozen)
- 1 banana
- 1 cup coconut water (or your choice of liquid)
- Ice cubes (optional)

Instructions:

1. In a blender, combine kale, pineapple, banana, and coconut water.
2. Blend until smooth. Add ice cubes for a colder smoothie if desired.
3. Serve immediately, garnished with a pineapple slice or a few kale leaves.

Honeydew Mint Smoothie

Ingredients:

- 1 cup honeydew melon, cubed
- 1/2 cup Greek yogurt (or your choice of yogurt)
- 1/2 cup almond milk (or your choice of milk)
- A few fresh mint leaves
- Ice cubes (optional)

Instructions:

1. In a blender, combine honeydew, yogurt, almond milk, and mint leaves.
2. Blend until smooth. Add ice cubes for a chilled smoothie if desired.
3. Serve immediately, garnished with a sprig of mint or honeydew slices.

Nutty Banana Oatmeal Smoothie

Ingredients:

- 1 banana
- 1/2 cup rolled oats
- 1 tablespoon almond butter (or your choice of nut butter)
- 1 cup almond milk (or your choice of milk)
- 1 tablespoon honey or maple syrup (optional)

Instructions:

1. In a blender, combine banana, rolled oats, almond butter, almond milk, and honey or maple syrup if using.
2. Blend until smooth. Add more milk for a thinner consistency if desired.
3. Serve immediately, garnished with banana slices or a sprinkle of oats.

Matcha Berry Smoothie

Ingredients:

- 1 cup mixed berries (fresh or frozen)
- 1 banana
- 1 cup almond milk (or your choice of milk)
- 1 teaspoon matcha green tea powder
- 1 tablespoon honey or maple syrup (optional)

Instructions:

1. In a blender, combine mixed berries, banana, almond milk, matcha powder, and honey or maple syrup if using.
2. Blend until smooth. Adjust sweetness if desired.
3. Serve immediately, garnished with a few whole berries or a sprinkle of matcha powder.

Enjoy these refreshing and nutritious smoothies!

www.ingramcontent.com/pod-product-compliance
Lightning Source LLC
LaVergne TN
LVHW081503060526
838201LV00056BA/2917